This book belongs to:

Rosie

HOW TO BE THE BEST BUBBLE WRITER IN THE WORLD EVER!

Published in 2011 by
Laurence King Publishing Ltd
361 – 373 City Road
London EC1V 1LR
United Kingdom
Tel: +44 20 7841 6900
Fax: +44 20 7841 6910
e-mail: enquiries@laurenceking.com
www.laurenceking.com

A catalogue record for this book is available from the British Library

ISBN: 978-1-85669-761-3

Commissioning Editor: Helen Rochester
Design: Mark Holt
Printed in China

HOW TO BE THE BEST BUBBLE WRITER IN THE WORLD EVER!

By Linda Scott

LAURENCE KING PUBLISHING

This book...

is here to change your life. Well, maybe not ALL of your life but definitely the bits that involve making posters, designing logos, creating your band name or pretty much ANYTHING in this lovely world that needs fun words, cool words and words that just HAVE to catch your eye.

If you don't know what 'bubble writing' is, it's hand-drawn letters that look a little, well, 'bubbly' and can be developed into almost any creative style that you can think of.

Sure, computers are great, but there's something sad about an alphabet that's been made by someone somewhere who isn't me...or now you.

Bubble writing IS big, it IS clever and it's just about the most fun you can have with a pen. I'm sure that once you start bubble writing you won't be able to stop. You can do it pretty much anytime and anywhere. Napkins, envelopes, letters, sketch books...they will all fall under the spell of your bubble writing habit.

If you enjoy using this book half as much as I have enjoyed making it, then you're in for a LOT of FUN. In fact I can pretty much guarantee that this book WILL MAKE YOU HAPPIER.

So dive in, be brave and get ready to enjoy yourself.

Welcome to my world!
The Bubble Writer

Remember - the rules are THERE ARE NO RULES.

Getting started

O.K. here we go!

In order to create the bubble writing alphabets in this book all you will need is a pencil, a blue ballpoint pen, a black felt-tip pen and an eraser. That's it.
However, to make each page your own I suggest that you collect some marker pens, grab some glitter and get hold of a stash of stickers. The more of your own marks that you make in this book, the more it will become yours.

Grab a sketchbook too. I love to use graph paper notebooks - the little squares on the graph paper really help to keep your letters looking neat and they will keep away the terror that is ... THE RULER.
Keep it in the drawer. Forever.

A ruler stops your letters from looking handmade, which is really what this is about. It doesn't matter if your letters are squiggly, wobbly, shaky or shy. They will be YOURS, they will be ORIGINAL and they will be UNIQUE - if you can read them, they're a success.

Try writing with any pens and pencils you can get your hands on - different tools will make your bubble writing look completely different.

Like most things that are worth doing, bubble writing can be tricky when you start, but just keep on trying. Each time you give an alphabet a go you will get braver, faster and better.

Remember, the rules are THERE ARE NO RULES.

Let's do it!

Best place to start? At the beginning. There are four alphabets that I call 'the basics'. It's a good idea to master these ones first. Pretty much all the other alphabets in the book follow on from the basic styles – with some twists and flourishes along the way!

So, let's look at **Freestyle**. Start by writing in your natural handwriting style in pencil. Next, draw an outline around the letters in pencil. When you are happy with them, go over in pen, like this:

At this stage you can rub out the pencil and fill the letters in, or keep them as outlines. What about adding some movement, hair or shine to really make it come alive? Like this:

The next one to try is **Basic Block**. This works in pretty much the same way as **Freestyle** but it's a little more important to keep the letters the same size and quite neat. Try doing this on graph or lined paper first.

What are the rules? THERE ARE NO RULES.

Next you can rub out the pencil lines and, same as before, fill the letters in or keep them as outlines. Try filling each letter with a different pattern and give it an interesting outline to create your own unique style.

Next comes the **3D Shaded Block**.
Start with a **Basic Block** outline and add depth to the letters by drawing lines from each corner – the same length and in the same direction. Next, mirror the letter shapes by joining the little lines up. Fill in the depth with stripes or a solid shade.

You can make the depth of the letters go in any direction and any size. Why not take all the depth lines off to one point in the distance for a real 'Superhero' look?

Hey, you know the rules don't you? THERE ARE NONE.

Feeling happy yet?

BUBBLEWRITER is a really fun alphabet to learn. Draw your letters as you did for **Freestyle**, but make them really fat and with nicely curved edges. Soft and squidgy looking is the name of the game! As you write the letters try to overlap them a bit. Like this:

When you are happy with the outline then rub out all the lines that you don't need, INCLUDING the lines of the letters that overlap ... but remember, just rub out one side of each of these overlapping letters. Add some shading to help the letters look more 3D.

Let your imagination go wild now and add some color, movement, patterns and decorations, and away you go. There is no end to the crazy bubble letters that you can now make!

Now go ahead and MAKE YOUR OWN RULES.

BUBBLEWRITER

A CLASSIC !!!

"ABCDEFGHIJ"
KLMNOPQRS
TUVWXYZ !?

Basic Outline

Practice this until you can do it in your sleep!

"Aa Bb Cc Dd Ee Ff Gg
Hh Ii Jj Kk Ll Mm Nn
Oo Pp Qq Rr Ss Tt Uu
Vv Ww Xx Yy Zz !?"

freestyle

make this one your signature ...

Rosie   Rosie   Rosie

!a b c d e f g h i
j k l m n o p q r
s t u v „w x y z „?

Basic 3D block

Practice makes perfect

"AaBb Cc Dd EeFf Gg
HhIiJjKk LlMmNn
OoPpQqRrSsTtUuVv
WwXxYyZz!?"

Let's have a look at some
really crazy and creative
bubble writing alphabets
now ... this first bunch are all
creatures and characters!

Turn the page and get
ready to be amazed!

Idea!
Why not start a box to collect scrap
papers in?
Envelopes, old cards, paper bags ... bubble
writing looks great on pretty much
anything!

hairy monster

What's your idea of scary?

66

_____
_____
_____

_____
_____
_____

_____
_____

_____
_____

_____
_____

_____
_____

99
_____
_____

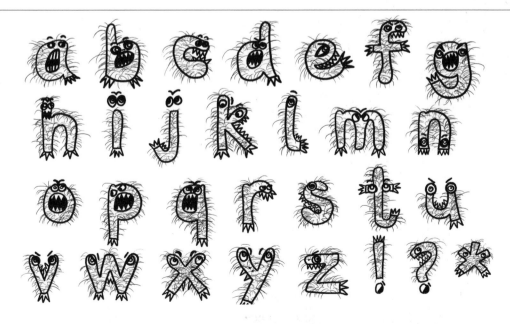

yeti

what does a yeti look like?

_____

_____
_____

_____
_____

_____
_____

_____
_____

_____

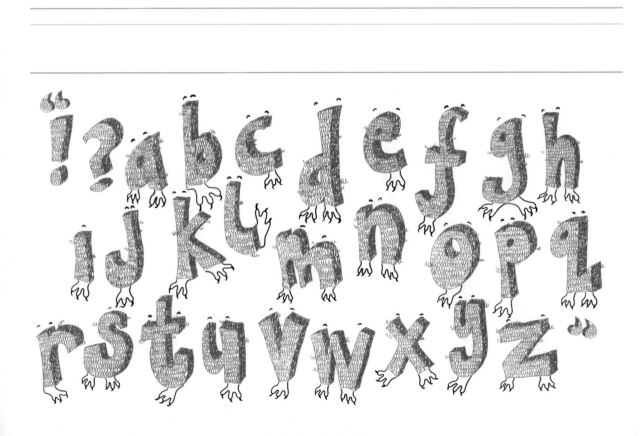

blob monster

can you make some more cute monsters?

_____

_____

_____

_____

_____

_____

_____

_____

_____

_____

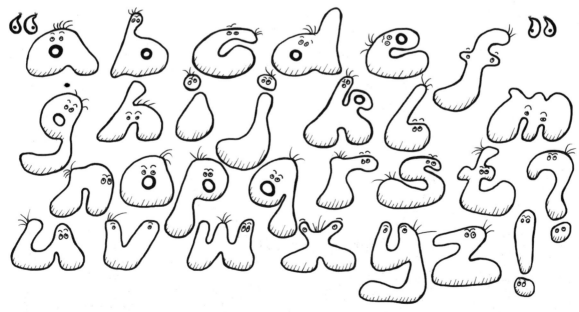

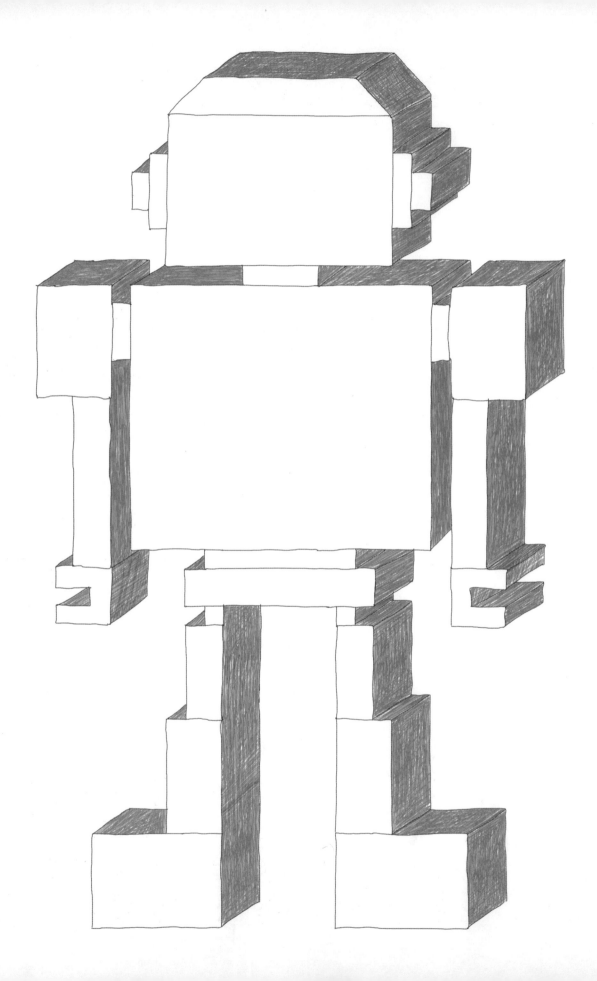

ROBOTS
IS THIS ROBOT FRIENDLY?

_____

_____

_____

_____

_____

_____

_____

_____

_____

_____

_____

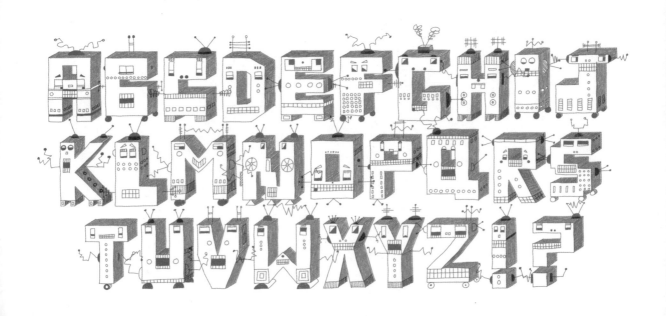

total crazy!
just go crazy...

" abcdefgh
klmnopq
uvwxyz "

supermouths
make some smiles today!!

Here are some activities for you to try with the bubble writing alphabets that you now know ...
Friendship notes, greeting cards, envelope stickers.
Color them in, cut them out, add some of your own ideas, then give them to someone fabulous!

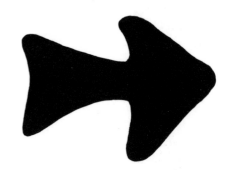

Idea!
Why not photocopy these pages before you draw on them?
That way you can do the activities over and over again.

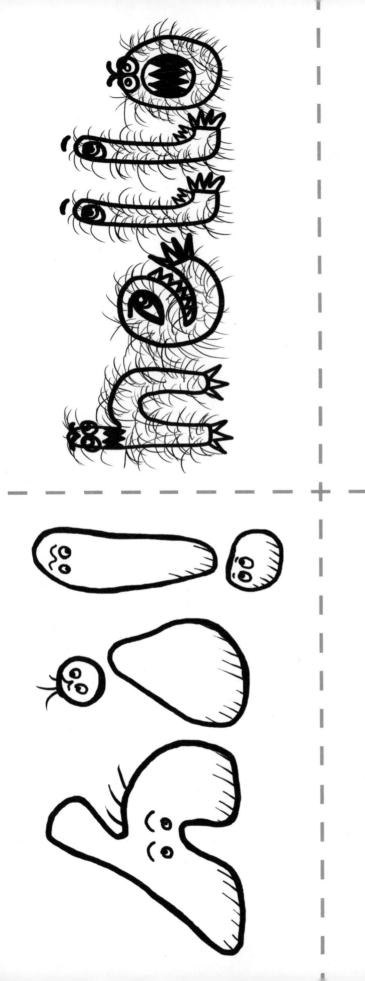
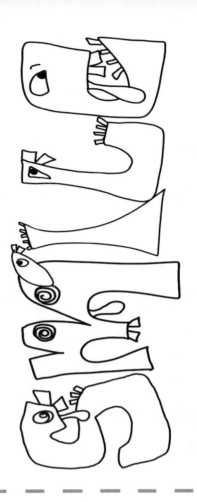

Here's a little friendship note for you...

Here's a little friendship note for you...

Here's a little friendship note for you...

Here's a little friendship note for you...

Here's an envelope label:
Cut it out and stick it onto
the front of an old envelope
to write the address on!
Reuse and recycle!

Woo hoo!... Love the trees!

Here's an envelope label:
Cut it out and stick it onto
the front of an old envelope
to write the address on!
Reuse and recycle!

Woo hoo!... Love the trees!

Here's an envelope label:
Cut it out and stick it onto
the front of an old envelope
to write the address on!
Reuse and recycle!

Woo hoo!... Love the trees!

Here's an envelope label:
Cut it out and stick it onto
the front of an old envelope
to write the address on!
Reuse and recycle!

Woo hoo!... Love the trees!

Here's a little friendship note for you...

Here's a little friendship note for you...

Here's a little friendship note for you...

Here's a little friendship note for you...

Here's an envelope label;
Cut it out and stick it onto
the front of an old envelope
to write the address on!
Reuse and recycle!

Woo hoo!... Love the trees!

Here's an envelope label;
Cut it out and stick it onto
the front of an old envelope
to write the address on!
Reuse and recycle!

Woo hoo!... Love the trees!

Here's an envelope label;
Cut it out and stick it onto
the front of an old envelope
to write the address on!
Reuse and recycle!

Woo hoo!... Love the trees!

Here's an envelope label;
Cut it out and stick it onto
the front of an old envelope
to write the address on!
Reuse and recycle!

Woo hoo!... Love the trees!

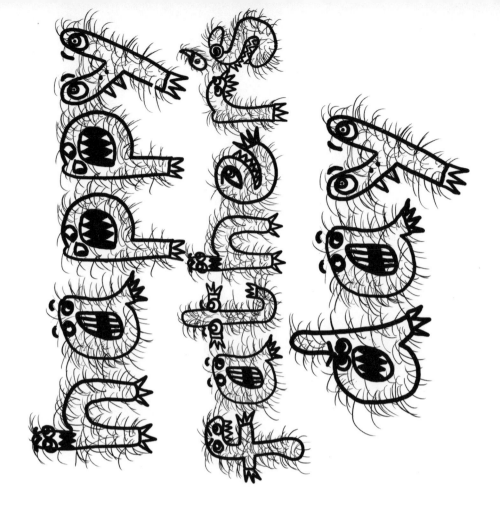

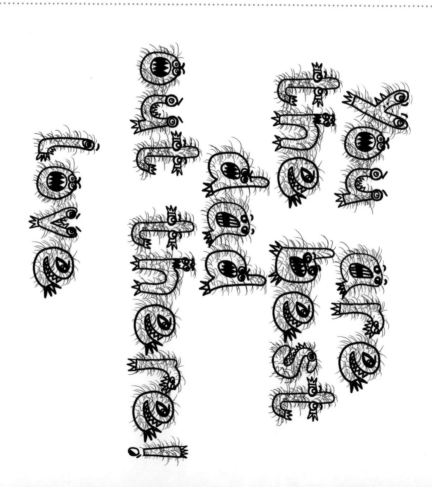

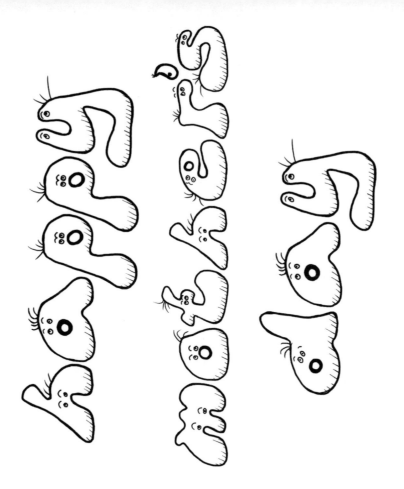

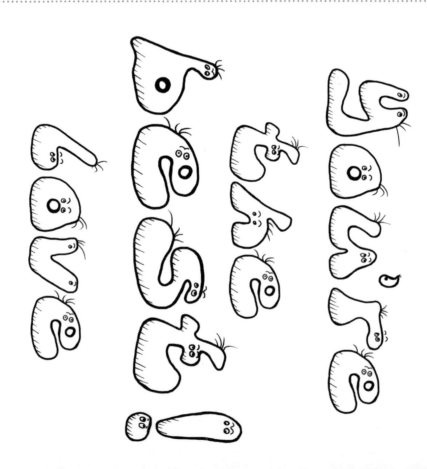

2

From

O.K.
Here are some more
bubble writing
alphabets for you
to learn – inspired
by all the kinds of
stuff that we see
around us all the
time!

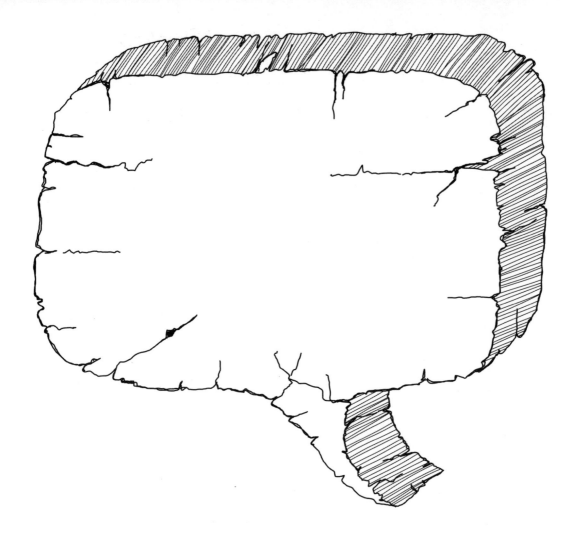

CAVEMAN

IMAGINE WHAT A CAVEMAN WOULD SAY

" ABCDEFG
HIJKLMN
OPQRSTU
VWXYZ!?"

skull n' crossbones

can you draw some more cool faces?

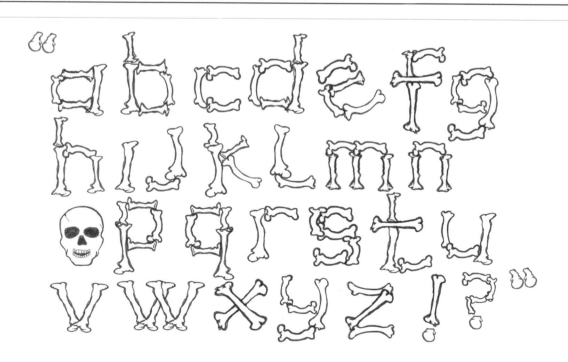

ROCK ON!

WHAT DO YOUR OWN ROCKIN' PATCHES LOOK LIKE?

ABCDEFGHI
JKLMNOPQR
STUVWXYZ !

ribbon

shade the ribbon

"abcdefghij
klmnopqr
stuvwxyz"

INKSPLAT

SPLAT SOME INK AND MAKE SOME FRIENDS!

" ABCDEFGHI !
JKLMNOPQR
STUVWXYZ?"

ghastly

try this with some chalk...

A a

Z z

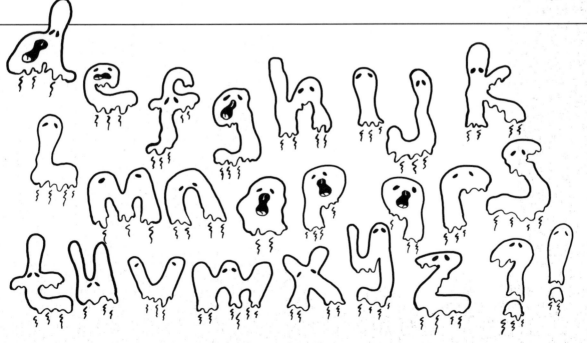

d e f g h i j k l m n o p q r s t u v w x y z ?!

Peacedoodle

doodling is so peaceful

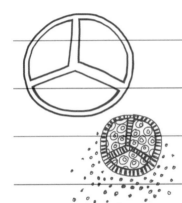

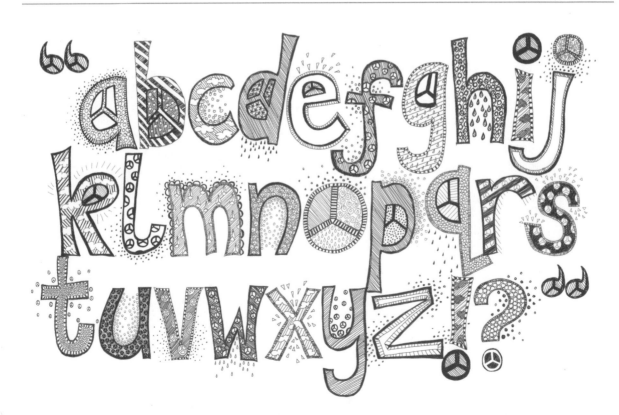

INVADERS

MAKE SOME LITTLE INVADERS OF YOUR OWN

" " A B C D E F G

H I J K L M N O

P Q R S T U V W

X Y Z ? ! . " "

Try your hand at making your own comic book adventure with the templates on the following pages ...
Use the bubble writing alphabets and characters that you have already learned.
(I've drawn a mini adventure page to show you the sort of thing that you could try.)

Tips:
Plan everything out in pencil before you commit to pen!
Why not use some of these speech bubbles on the next page? Copy them or cut them out and stick them down in the comic.

THE ADVENTURES OF BLOBERT...

In: The Magic Weather Umbrella

Blobert was having a really bad day...

IT WAS *windy* AND *rainy* AND VERY COLD

BUT THEN!

Luckily he found an umbrella on the ground.

WHEN BLOBERT PUT IT UP...

A magic spell came rushing out of the umbrella!

Hooray! Now I'm chillin' in the sun.

THE END

Now have a go at making your own comic adventure.

THE ADVENTURES

OF.........................

CONTINUED...

THE END

Ready for some more fantastic
bubble writing alphabets?
Then read on ...
These ones are all inspired by
nature.

Cloudabet

Draw some cloud shapes of your own...

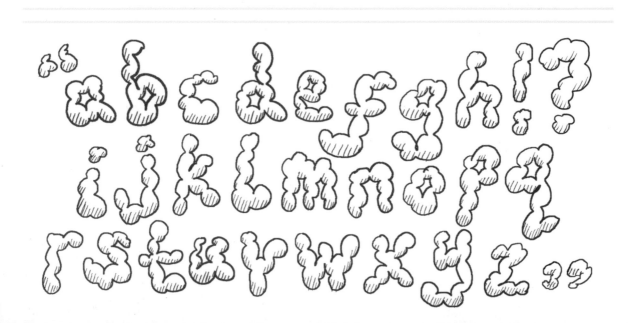

LIGHTNING STRIKE
MAKE A STORM !

"

"

? ABCDEFGHI
JKLMNOPQ !
RSTUVWXYZ

rainbow fun

brighten up the rainbow!

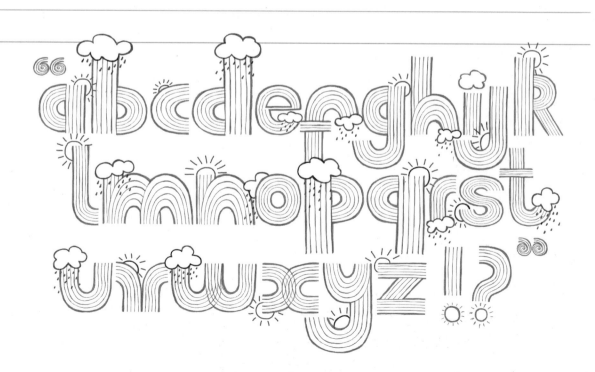

cact.us

what. Lives in the desert. ?

abcde.f.ghi
.jkl.mnopqr
st.uvwxyz?

Spooky Hollow

Add some spooky eyes...

"Aa Bb Cc Dd Ee Ff Gg
Hh Ii Jj Kk Ll Mm Nn
Oo Pp Qq Rr Ss Tt Uu
Vv Ww Xx Yy Zz ! ?"

SHOOTIN' STARS

CONTINUE WITH THE SHOOTIN' STARS PATTERN...

A B C D E F G H I

J K L M N O P Q

R S T U V W X Y Z

MOUNTAIN SPEAK

I SEE A COUPLE OF BALD ONES!

_____

_____

_____

_____

_____

_____

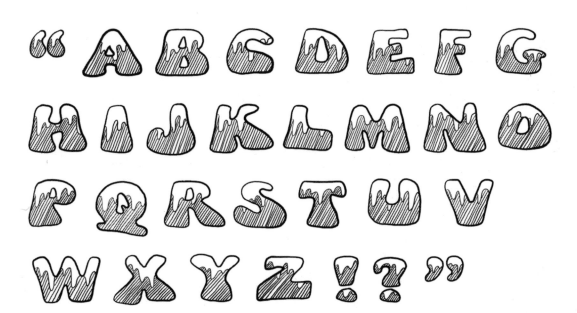

" A B C D E F G
H I J K L M N O
P Q R S T U V
W X Y Z ! ? ? "

Groovy contours

finish the land and think of
a name for it ...

"a b c d e f g
h i j k l m n
o p q r s t u
v w x y z ! ? "

Over the next few pages you will find some amazing ideas of things to make with all your new bubble writing alphabets ... and some things for you to finish off and draw for yourself.

What else can you think of to make with your funky new writing?

Tip:
If you are having a party why not photocopy the party invites enough times for ALL the friends you'd like to come?

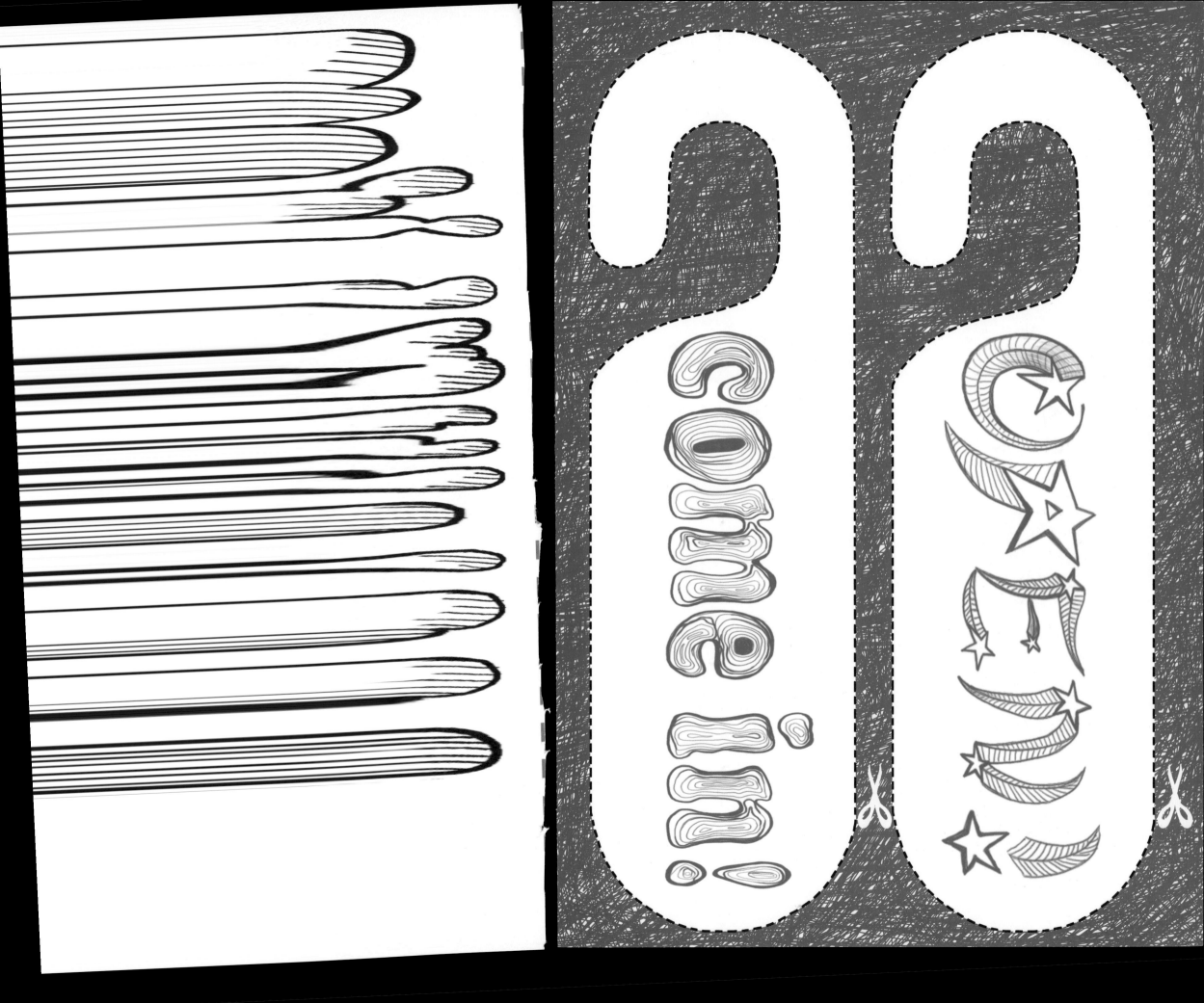

CLOSE

STAY AWAY!

this book belongs to ...

Think of some welcoming words for these door hangers...

...what about some not so welcoming words?

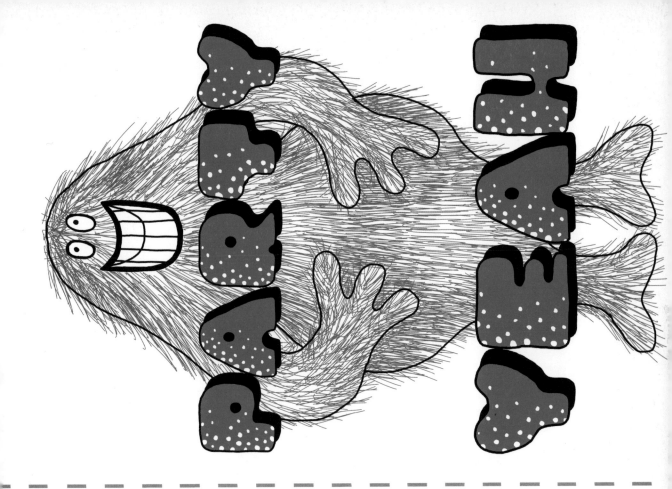

Please come to my party!

When ·····

Where ·····

What time ·····

RSVP ·····

From ·····

Please come to my party!

When ·····

Where ·····

What time ·····

RSVP ·····

From ·····

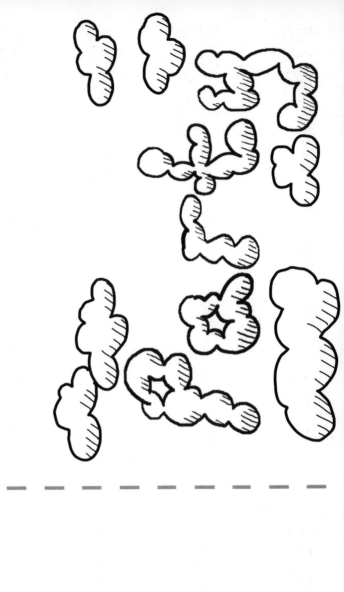

Please come to my party!

When ....

Where ....

What time ....

RSVP ....

From ....

Please come to my party!

When ....

Where ....

What time ....

RSVP ....

From ....

If you have something amazing to say you could write it in this speech bubble and put it somewhere for everyone to see!

Say something amazing every day!

Make your own party invitations ...

... anything goes!

...really, anything goes!

Take a look over the next few pages...

Here are more bubble alphabets, this time inspired (mostly) by the seasons and the time.

TIP:
Make today a 'change your pen day'... and see what your bubble writing looks like just by changing what you write with!

DAY CITY

IMAGINE A CITY IN YOUR DAYDREAMS

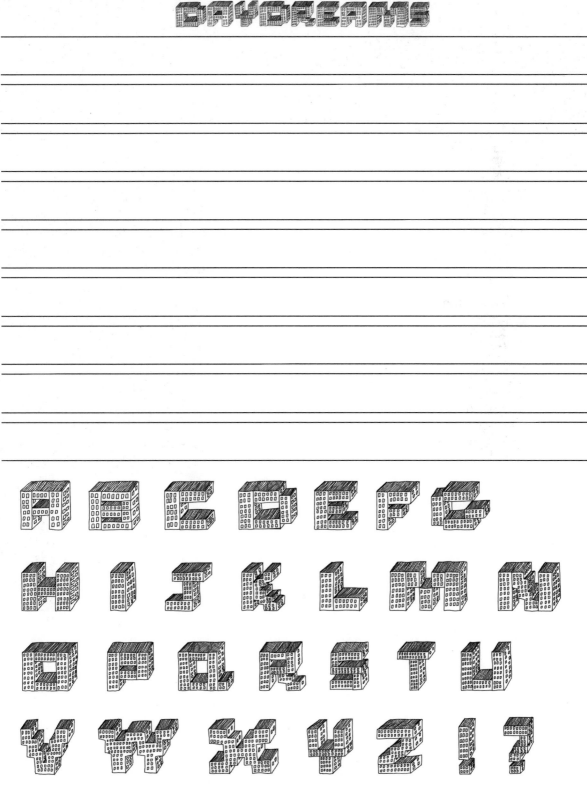

NIGHT CITY
AND YOUR NIGHTMARES...

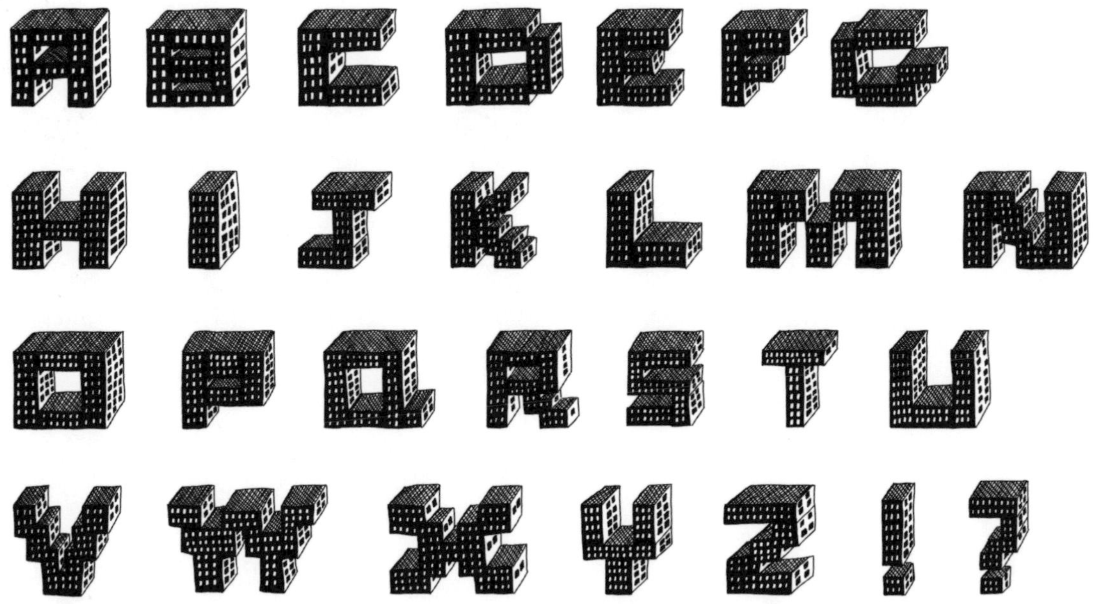

_____

_____

_____

_____

_____

_____

_____

_____

_____

_____

_____

_____

A B C D E F G
H I J K L M N
O P Q R S T U
V W X Y Z ! ?

snowman

build some snowpeople,
whatever the weather

VALENTINE

DRAWING HEARTS ALL DAY IS, QUITE
FRANKLY, GOOD FOR YOUR HEART

"ABCDEFGHIJ
KLMNOPQRS
TUVWXYZ!?"

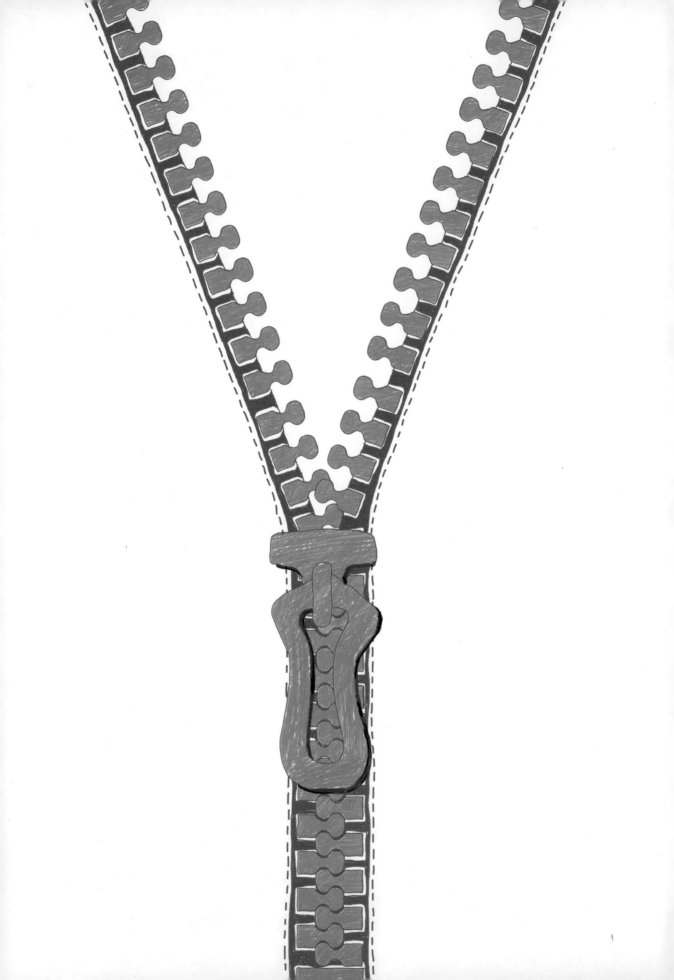

"ZIP IT!"

I LOVE SUMMER CAMPING...
WHAT'S THROUGH THIS TENT ZIP?

_____

_____

_____

_____

_____

ABCDEFGHIJ
KLMNOPQRS
TUVWXYZ!?

HALLOWEEN
CARVE SOME MORE SCARY PUMPKIN FACES....

PRESENTS

WRAP SOME MORE!

ABCDEFGHIJ
KLMNOPQRS
TUVWXYZ!?

Summer Cakes

add Some Sprinkles

"

"

Here are some templates to write letters with the bubble writing alphabets that you have learned.

Cut them out, write the letter, glue them down into envelopes, send them to someone special.

Hey ... everyone loves to get a letter in the post!

cut along the dashed lines

fold along the dotted lines

DEAR

LOVE FROM

cut along the dashed lines

fold along the dotted lines

glue here after folding

glue here after folding

glue here after folding

glue here after folding

dear

fold along the dotted lines

love from

cut along the dashed lines

fold along the dotted lines

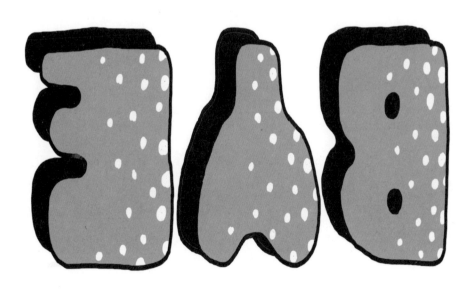

HELLO

LOVE FROM

DEAR

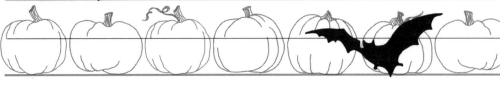

LOVE FROM

Here are the last few alphabets... now go out there and be a great bubble writer!

Question:
Are you still saving all the paper that you can find?
Bubble writing isn't just for inside this book – bubble write every day, on everything that you can!

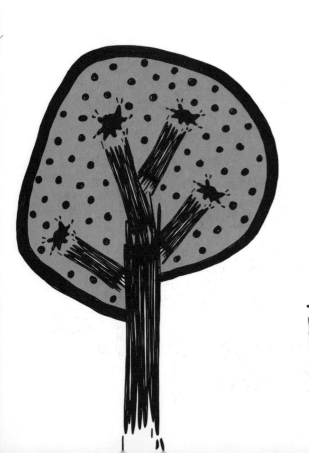

brushstroke

what can you make with a brushstroke?

T

"abcdefg
hijklmno
pqrstuv
wxyz!?"

GRAFFITI

LEARN TO WRITE YOUR NAME!

ABCDEFGHI
JKLMNOPQRST
UVWXYZ &

SLIME

"ALMOST FINISHED!"

A B C D E F G H I
J K L M N O P Q R
S T U V W X Y Z

Create your own alphabet here ...

(Think of a cool name for it here) ↑

...and another one here...

((Can you give it a fun name here?) ↑

If you make an alphabet that you want to share, go to www.bubblewriter.com to find out how.

I really hope that you've enjoyed this book!

I had a lot of fun making it for you. Bubble writing is like an itch to me – and one that I just keep having to scratch! I use it all the time – on posters, things to do lists, T-shirt prints, cool letters for friends... bubble writing even helped to find my cat when he was lost by making a really eye-catching poster!

It's an amazingly fun thing to do and there are LOADS of great people out there doing it. If you need more inspiration just put 'hand-drawn type' or 'handmade letters' into a search engine and see what comes up. And look around at all the letters you see every day. You probably see many more than you realize.

If you make an alphabet that you love, why not turn it into a font (like this one) for you, your friends and family to use on their computers – it's a GREAT way of mixing technology with drawing by hand! Check out www.yourfonts.com. It's pretty simple to do and not expensive.

I designed all the alphabets in this book EXCEPT for Graffiti – I am not a graffiti expert but thought that you would really like a graffiti alphabet. The font I used is called Graffonti 3D Drop and I found it on a great FREE FONTS website called www.dafont.com. There are lots of free font websites online, so have a good look around.

Remember, be happy and have fun when you are making letters – it will show! Keep in mind that your letters are SUPPOSED to look hand-drawn. That's the point.

I hope that this book will inspire you to become one of the most creative and original bubble writers out there!

The Bubble Writer

Remember...

MAKE WORDS NOT WAR

this is not the end this is just the beginning

Thanks
so much for all of your
help in making this book!

Mick, Harvey, Bonnie, Jim, Sheena, Fiona, Zakee, Peter F, Lucie and Jim, Charlotte and Joey, Robyn and Karen, Sophie and Rachel, Charlotte over the road, and Jess.